What Is an Insect?

by Lola M. Schaefer

ground beetle

Consulting Editor: Gail Saunders-Smith, Ph.D.

Consultant: Gary A. Dunn, Director of Education,
Young Entomologists' Society

Pebble Books

an imprint of Capstone Press
Mankato, Minnesota

Pebble Books are published by Capstone Press
151 Good Counsel Drive, P.O. Box 669, Mankato, Minnesota 56002
http://www.capstone-press.com

1 2 3 4 5 6 06 05 04 03 02 01

Library of Congress Cataloging-in-Publication Data
Schaefer, Lola M., 1950–
    What is an insect?/by Lola M. Schaefer.
    p. cm.—(The Animal Kingdom)
    Includes bibliographical references (p. 23) and index.
    ISBN 0-7368-0866-3
    1. Insects—Juvenile literature. [1. Insects.] I. Title. II. Series.
QL467.2 .S33 2001
595.7—dc21   00-009671

Summary: Simple text and photographs describe and illustrate kinds of insects and
their characteristics.

Note to Parents and Teachers

The Animal Kingdom series supports national science standards
related to the diversity of life. This book describes the characteristics
of insects and illustrates various kinds of insects. The photographs
support early readers in understanding the text. The repetition of
words and phrases helps early readers learn new words. This book
also introduces early readers to subject-specific vocabulary words,
which are defined in the Words to Know section. Early readers may
need assistance to read some words and to use the Table of
Contents, Words to Know, Read More, Internet Sites, and
Index/Word List sections of the book.

Table of Contents

Insects are part of
the animal kingdom.
They are among
the smallest animals.

swallowtail butterfly

exoskeleton

Insects have
an exoskeleton.

ladybug

head

thorax

abdomen

Insects have
three main body parts.

velvet ant wasp

Insects have
two large eyes.

house fly

mouthparts

Insects have mouthparts.

ant

antennas

Insects have two antennas.

short-horned grasshopper

16

Insects have six legs.

camel cricket

Most insects have
wings and can fly.

white-tailed dragonfly

Female insects lay eggs.
Millions of young insects
hatch every day.

young praying mantises

Words to Know

animal kingdom—the group that includes all animals; the animal kingdom is one of the three kingdoms that includes all living things; the other two kingdoms are the plant kingdom and the mineral kingdom.

antenna—a feeler on an insect's head; most insects use their antennas to touch, taste, or smell.

body—all the parts that a person or animal is made of; the main body parts of an insect are a head, a thorax, and an abdomen.

exoskeleton—the tough or stiff structure on the outside of some animals; the exoskeleton covers and protects the animal.

female—an animal that can give birth to young animals or lay eggs

insect—a small animal with an exoskeleton, three body parts, six legs, and two antennas; about 1 million kinds of insects have been named in the world so far.

Read More

Berger, Melvin. *Buzz!: A Book about Insects.* Hello Science Reader! New York: Scholastic, 2000.

Canizares, Susan, and Mary Reid. *What Is an Insect?* Science Emergent Readers. New York: Scholastic, 1998.

Stone, Lynn M. *What Makes an Insect?* Animal Kingdom. Vero Beach, Fla.: Rourke, 1997.

Internet Sites

Animals of the World
http://www.kidscom.com/orakc/Games/
Animalgame/index.html

Bugbios
http://www.insects.org

Insects
http://www.EnchantedLearning.com/
subjects/insects/printouts.shtml

Index/Word List

Word Count: 57
Early-Intervention Level: 7

Editorial Credits
Mari C. Schuh, editor; Kia Bielke, designer; Kimberly Danger, photo researcher

Photo Credits
Bob Gossington/Bruce Coleman Inc, 8
Digital Stock, cover (upper left)
Dwight R. Kuhn, cover (lower left and lower right), 6
George Forrest Sr./Bruce Coleman Inc., 14
J. C. Carton/Bruce Coleman Inc., 1
Laura Riley/Bruce Coleman Inc., 20
Photo Network/Robert Grubbs, 18
Robert & Linda Mitchell, cover (upper right), 10, 12
Visuals Unlimited/Robert Clay, 4; G. and C. Merker, 16